JOHNNY MARSHALL

FROM DEBT TO DREAMS:

Creating Financial Freedom

Through Smart Money

Management

A Concise Guide

Copyright.

All rights reserved. No part of this publication may be republished in any form or by any means without written permission from the author.

INTRODUCTION	6
CHAPTER 1	9
INTRODUCTION: FROM DEBT TO DREAMS - THE PATH TO FINANCIAL FREEDOM	9
CHAPTER 2	13
ASSESSING YOUR CURRENT FINANCIAL SITUATION	13
CHAPTER 3	17
CREATING A REALISTIC BUDGET	17
CHAPTER 4	20
DEBT MANAGEMENT STRATEGIES	20
CHAPTER 5	23
BUILDING AN EMERGENCY FUND	23
CHAPTER 6	26
SAVING FOR SHORT-TERM AND LONG-TERM GOALS	26
CHAPTER 7	29
THE POWER OF FRUGALITY AND MINDFUL SPENDING	29

CHAPTER 8	**32**
INCREASING YOUR INCOME STREAMS	**32**
CHAPTER 9	**35**
UNDERSTANDING CREDIT AND BUILDING A POSITIVE CREDIT HISTORY	**35**
CHAPTER 10	**38**
SAVING FOR RETIREMENT	**38**
CHAPTER 11	**41**
ESTATE PLANNING AND PROTECTING YOUR ASSETS	**41**
CHAPTER 12	**44**
PROTECTING YOUR FINANCIAL WELL-BEING WITH INSURANCE	**44**
CHAPTER 13	**47**
INVESTING FOR WEALTH CREATION	**47**
CHAPTER 14	**50**
TAX PLANNING STRATEGIES FOR FINANCIAL OPTIMIZATION	**50**

CHAPTER 15   53

MINDSET SHIFT: CULTIVATING A POSITIVE RELATIONSHIP WITH MONEY   53

CHAPTER 16   56

FINANCIAL EDUCATION FOR CHILDREN AND TEENS   56

CHAPTER 17   59

NAVIGATING MAJOR LIFE EVENTS: FINANCIAL CONSIDERATIONS   59

CHAPTER 18   62

PHILANTHROPY AND GIVING BACK: THE POWER OF GENEROSITY   62

CHAPTER 19   65

FINANCIAL SECURITY FOR AN UNCERTAIN FUTURE   65

CHAPTER 20   68

FINANCIAL SUCCESS AS A JOURNEY, NOT A DESTINATION   68

INTRODUCTION

In today's world, achieving financial freedom has become a universal aspiration. The path to this freedom starts with smart money management, which allows individuals to transform their lives from being burdened by debt to pursuing their dreams. This book, "From Debt to Dreams," serves as a comprehensive guide to help readers navigate the complexities of personal finance and develop the skills necessary to take control of their financial destiny. By delving into topics such as budgeting, debt management, saving, investing, and retirement planning, this book empowers readers to make informed decisions and develop a roadmap towards financial freedom. Through practical strategies, valuable insights, and actionable steps, readers will learn how to break free from the shackles of debt, build a strong financial foundation, and ultimately create a life filled with endless possibilities.

"From Debt to Dreams" presents a holistic approach to money management, addressing not only the practical aspects of budgeting and investing but also the mindset and habits necessary for long-term financial success. The book highlights the importance of frugality, mindful spending, and increasing income streams to accelerate debt repayment and savings growth. It also emphasizes the significance of protecting one's financial well-being through insurance and estate planning. With a focus on fostering a positive money mindset, the book helps readers overcome limiting beliefs and develop healthy financial habits. It also encourages readers to impart financial literacy to their children and future generations, ensuring a legacy of financial empowerment. By the end of this transformative journey, readers will have the tools, knowledge, and confidence to achieve financial freedom, turning their dreams into tangible realities.

CHAPTER 1
INTRODUCTION: FROM DEBT TO DREAMS - THE PATH TO FINANCIAL FREEDOM

Section 1: Exploring the importance of smart money management. In this section, we delve into the significance of smart money management and how it can profoundly impact an individual's life. We discuss how poor financial management can lead to overwhelming debt, stress, and limited opportunities, while effective money management can pave the way to a brighter future. By understanding the value of each dollar earned, individuals can make conscious choices that align with their long-term goals and aspirations. We emphasize that achieving financial freedom is not just about accumulating wealth but also about gaining control over one's financial situation, reducing stress, and creating a sense of security.

Section 2: Understanding the link between debt and dreams Here, we explore the relationship between debt and the ability to pursue one's dreams. We discuss how excessive debt can act as a roadblock, preventing individuals from fulfilling their aspirations and living life on their own terms. We examine the various forms of debt, such as credit card debt, student loans, and mortgages, and the impact they can have on financial freedom. By understanding the consequences of debt, readers will gain motivation and inspiration to take control of their financial situation and break free from the chains of indebtedness.

Section 3: Setting financial goals for a brighter future. In this section, we emphasize the importance of setting clear financial goals as a crucial step towards achieving financial freedom. We guide readers through the process of identifying their dreams, both short-term and long-term, and translating them into tangible financial objectives. By setting specific, measurable, achievable, relevant, and time-bound

(SMART) goals, readers can gain clarity and direction in their financial journey. We provide practical tips and strategies to help readers develop an action plan that aligns with their goals, whether it's becoming debt-free, saving for a dream vacation, starting a business, or planning for retirement. By the end of this section, readers will be equipped with the tools and motivation to embark on their path to financial freedom.

CHAPTER 2
ASSESSING YOUR CURRENT FINANCIAL SITUATION

Section 1: Conducting a comprehensive review of your income and expenses. In this section, we guide readers through the process of conducting a thorough assessment of their current financial situation. We provide tools and worksheets to help them track their income from various sources and categorize their expenses. By analysing their spending patterns, readers gain valuable insights into where their money is going and can identify areas where they can potentially cut back or make adjustments to achieve better financial balance.

Section 2: Tracking your spending habits and identifying areas for improvement Here, we dive deeper into the importance of tracking spending habits. We provide practical tips on how to use budgeting apps, spreadsheets, or other tools to monitor expenses effectively. By understanding their spending habits, readers can identify areas where they may be overspending or making unnecessary purchases. We also emphasize the importance of distinguishing between needs and wants, and how aligning spending with priorities can lead to significant savings.

Section 3: Calculating your net worth and understanding your financial standing. In this section, we explore the concept of net worth and its significance in evaluating overall financial health. We guide readers through the process of calculating their net worth by subtracting their liabilities (debts) from their assets. By understanding their net worth, readers gain a clear picture of their current financial standing and can set realistic goals for improvement. We also discuss strategies to increase net worth, such as debt reduction and increasing assets through saving and investing.

CHAPTER 3
CREATING A REALISTIC BUDGET

Section 1: Establishing a budgeting framework that suits your lifestyle. Here, we discuss various budgeting methods and help readers choose a framework that aligns with their lifestyle and financial goals. We explore popular budgeting approaches such as the 50/30/20 rule, zero-based budgeting, and envelope budgeting. By selecting a budgeting system that resonates with them, readers can establish a solid foundation for managing their income and expenses effectively.

Section 2: Allocating funds for essential expenses, savings, and debt repayment. In this section, we provide guidance on how to allocate funds within a budget. We emphasize the importance of prioritizing essential expenses such as housing, utilities, and groceries, while also setting aside money for savings and debt repayment. We offer practical tips on budgeting for irregular expenses, emergencies, and future goals to ensure a well-rounded financial plan.

Section 3: Implementing strategies to stick to your budget and avoid overspending Here, we explore strategies to help readers stick to their budget and resist the temptation to overspend. We discuss techniques such as setting spending limits, practicing mindful spending, and tracking progress regularly. We also address common challenges and provide tips on overcoming budgeting hurdles, such as dealing with impulsive purchases, managing lifestyle inflation, and finding accountability partners.

CHAPTER 4
DEBT MANAGEMENT STRATEGIES

Section 1: Evaluating different types of debt and their impact on your financial freedom. In this section, we delve into the different types of debt that individuals may encounter, including credit card debt, student loans, mortgages, and personal loans. We discuss the potential consequences of carrying high levels of debt, such as high-interest charges, limited borrowing capacity, and reduced financial flexibility. By understanding the impact of debt on financial freedom, readers are motivated to take proactive steps towards managing and reducing their debts.

Section 2: Developing a debt repayment plan and prioritizing high-interest debts. Here, we guide readers through the process of creating a debt repayment plan. We discuss various strategies, such as the snowball method and avalanche method, for prioritizing and tackling debts. We provide practical tips on negotiating with creditors, exploring debt consolidation options, and making consistent payments to accelerate debt repayment.

Section 3: Exploring debt consolidation and negotiation options. In this section, we delve deeper into debt consolidation and negotiation options. We discuss the pros and cons of consolidating multiple debts into a single loan or balance transfer credit card. We also explore negotiation strategies for reducing interest rates, settling debts for less than the full amount owed, or setting up manageable repayment plans. By understanding these options, readers can make informed decisions to streamline their debt repayment process.

CHAPTER 5
BUILDING AN EMERGENCY FUND

Section 1: Understanding the importance of having a financial safety net. In this section, we emphasize the significance of having an emergency fund as a crucial component of financial freedom. We discuss unexpected expenses and the potential consequences of not having a financial safety net. By understanding the importance of an emergency fund, readers are motivated to prioritize saving and establish a buffer against unforeseen circumstances.

Section 2: Setting savings goals and creating a plan to build an emergency fund Here, we guide readers through the process of setting savings goals and developing a plan to build their emergency fund. We discuss the recommended amount for an emergency fund based on individual circumstances and provide strategies to increase savings. We also explore different savings vehicles, such as high-yield savings accounts or money market accounts, to maximize the growth of their emergency fund.

Section 3: Exploring strategies to save money and overcome common obstacles. In this section, we provide practical tips and strategies to help readers save money and overcome common obstacles that may hinder their savings progress. We discuss techniques such as automating savings, cutting expenses, negotiating bills, and finding creative ways to increase income. By implementing these strategies, readers can accelerate their savings and establish a robust emergency fund.

CHAPTER 6
SAVING FOR SHORT-TERM AND LONG-TERM GOALS

Section 1: Identifying short-term financial goals and creating a savings plan. In this section, we help readers identify and prioritize their short-term financial goals, such as a vacation, a down payment for a home, or purchasing a new vehicle. We guide them through the process of creating a savings plan that aligns with their goals, taking into account their timeline, income, and expenses. We also provide tips on how to stay motivated and track progress towards achieving these short-term goals.

Section 2: Exploring long-term goals such as retirement planning and education funding. Here, we shift focus to long-term financial goals, such as retirement planning and education funding. We discuss the importance of starting early and leveraging the power of compound interest. We explore different retirement accounts, such as 401(k)s and IRAs, and provide guidance on choosing appropriate investment vehicles. Additionally, we discuss strategies for saving and investing for education expenses, including 529 plans and education savings accounts.

Section 3: Understanding different investment options and their potential returns. In this section, we provide an overview of various investment options available to individuals seeking long-term growth. We explore the basics of stocks, bonds, mutual funds, exchange-traded funds (ETFs), and real estate investments. We discuss the risk-return trade-off and the importance of diversification. By understanding different investment vehicles and their potential returns, readers can make informed decisions about building wealth and achieving their long-term financial goals.

CHAPTER 7
THE POWER OF FRUGALITY AND MINDFUL SPENDING

Section 1: Embracing a frugal lifestyle and finding joy in simple pleasures. In this section, we delve into the concept of frugality and the power it holds in achieving financial freedom. We discuss how embracing a frugal lifestyle does not equate to deprivation but rather finding joy in simple pleasures and conscious spending. We provide practical tips on how to adopt frugal habits, such as meal planning, shopping mindfully, and embracing minimalism. By embracing frugality, readers can reduce unnecessary expenses and redirect their resources towards achieving their dreams.

Section 2: Overcoming common challenges and temptations in consumer culture Here, we address common challenges and temptations that individuals may face in a consumer-driven society. We discuss strategies to resist impulse purchases, navigate marketing tactics, and avoid lifestyle inflation. We also explore the psychology behind consumerism and provide guidance on cultivating contentment and gratitude to combat the desire for material possessions.

Section 3: Saving money on everyday expenses and maximizing value. In this section, we provide practical tips and strategies for saving money on everyday expenses without sacrificing quality of life. We discuss techniques such as comparison shopping, utilizing coupons and discounts, negotiating prices, and embracing do-it-yourself (DIY) projects. By implementing these strategies, readers can make their money go further and optimize their spending habits.

CHAPTER 8
INCREASING YOUR INCOME STREAMS

Section 1: Evaluating current income sources and identifying opportunities for growth. In this section, we guide readers through the process of evaluating their current income sources and identifying opportunities for growth. We discuss strategies such as asking for a raise, seeking promotions or career advancements, and exploring additional part-time or freelance work. By maximizing their earning potential, readers can accelerate their journey towards financial freedom.

Section 2: Exploring side hustles and entrepreneurial ventures Here, we delve into the world of side hustles and entrepreneurial ventures as a means to increase income. We discuss various side hustle ideas, such as freelance writing, tutoring, pet sitting, or starting an online business. We provide guidance on how to identify profitable opportunities, manage time effectively, and overcome common obstacles that may arise when pursuing additional income streams.

Section 3: Building passive income through investments and other sources. In this section, we explore the concept of passive income and its role in achieving financial freedom. We discuss different avenues for generating passive income, such as real estate investments, dividend-paying stocks, peer-to-peer lending, and royalties from creative works. We also provide insights on the potential risks and rewards associated with passive income streams. By diversifying income sources and incorporating passive income strategies, readers can create additional revenue streams that contribute to their financial goals.

CHAPTER 9
UNDERSTANDING CREDIT AND BUILDING A POSITIVE CREDIT HISTORY

Section 1: Exploring the importance of credit and its impact on financial opportunities. In this section, we delve into the importance of credit and how it impacts an individual's financial opportunities. We discuss how credit scores and credit reports are used by lenders, landlords, and employers to assess creditworthiness. We emphasize the significance of building and maintaining a positive credit history to access favourable loan terms, rental agreements, and employment opportunities.

Section 2: Navigating the world of credit cards and using them responsibly Here, we provide guidance on the responsible use of credit cards and maximizing their benefits. We discuss how to choose the right credit card, understand interest rates and fees, and develop healthy credit card habits. We also explore strategies for managing credit card debt, such as paying off balances in full, utilizing balance transfers, and avoiding high-interest charges.

Section 3: Building and improving credit through loans and other credit-building strategies. In this section, we discuss strategies for building and improving credit through responsible borrowing. We explore options such as secured credit cards, credit-builder loans, and authorized user arrangements. We also provide tips on how to establish a solid credit history, including making timely payments, keeping credit utilization low, and regularly monitoring credit reports. By understanding the factors that influence credit scores and implementing credit-building strategies, readers can enhance their financial opportunities and improve their overall financial health.

CHAPTER 10
SAVING FOR RETIREMENT

Section 1: Understanding the importance of retirement planning and compounding growth. In this section, we emphasize the importance of retirement planning and how starting early can significantly impact one's financial future. We discuss the power of compounding growth and how it can exponentially increase retirement savings over time. We provide insights into the potential costs of retirement and the significance of setting realistic retirement goals.

Section 2: Exploring retirement account options and maximizing contributions Here, we delve into different retirement account options, such as employer-sponsored 401(k)s, individual retirement accounts (IRAs), and Roth IRAs. We discuss the tax advantages, contribution limits, and investment opportunities associated with each account type. We also provide guidance on how to maximize contributions and leverage employer matching programs to accelerate retirement savings.

Section 3: Developing an investment strategy for retirement funds. In this section, we explore the importance of developing an investment strategy for retirement funds. We discuss asset allocation, diversification, and risk tolerance as key factors in constructing a retirement portfolio. We also provide an overview of investment options, such as target-date funds, index funds, and individual stocks, to help readers make informed investment decisions. By developing a tailored investment strategy, readers can optimize their retirement savings and increase the likelihood of a financially secure retirement.

CHAPTER 11
ESTATE PLANNING AND PROTECTING YOUR ASSETS

Section 1: Understanding the importance of estate planning for financial security. In this section, we discuss the significance of estate planning in protecting one's assets and ensuring a smooth transfer of wealth. We explore the components of an estate plan, including wills, trusts, powers of attorney, and healthcare directives. We emphasize the importance of proactive estate planning, regardless of age or wealth, to avoid potential complications and provide for loved ones.

Section 2: Navigating the legal aspects of estate planning Here, we provide an overview of the legal aspects of estate planning and guide readers through the process of creating essential estate planning documents. We discuss the role of attorneys, notaries, and other professionals in assisting with estate planning. We also address common concerns and considerations, such as guardianship for minor children, charitable giving, and minimizing estate taxes.

Section 3: Reviewing and updating your estate plan regularly. In this section, we stress the importance of reviewing and updating estate plans regularly to ensure they align with changing circumstances and goals. We discuss life events that may necessitate updates, such as marriage, divorce, births, deaths, or significant financial changes. By keeping their estate plans up to date, readers can maintain control over their assets and ensure their wishes are carried out according to their intentions.

CHAPTER 12
PROTECTING YOUR FINANCIAL WELL-BEING WITH INSURANCE

Section 1: Understanding the role of insurance in financial security. In this section, we explore the role of insurance in protecting one's financial well-being. We discuss different types of insurance coverage, such as health insurance, auto insurance, homeowner's insurance, life insurance, and disability insurance. We emphasize the importance of evaluating individual needs and selecting appropriate coverage to mitigate financial risks.

Section 2: Navigating the insurance landscape and making informed choices

Here, we provide guidance on navigating the insurance landscape and making informed choices when selecting insurance policies. We discuss factors to consider, such as coverage limits, deductibles, and premiums. We also explore options for comparing insurance quotes, leveraging discounts, and understanding policy terms and conditions. By understanding the fundamentals of insurance, readers can make educated decisions to protect their financial well-being.

Section 3: Evaluating and adjusting insurance coverage as circumstances change. In this section, we highlight the importance of regularly evaluating insurance coverage and adjusting policies as circumstances change. We discuss life events that may necessitate updates, such as marriage, divorce, home renovations, or changes in health status. We also emphasize the significance of revaluating coverage periodically to ensure it aligns with current needs and offers adequate protection.

CHAPTER 13
INVESTING FOR WEALTH CREATION

Section 1: Understanding the principles of investing and the power of compound growth. In this section, we introduce the principles of investing and the concept of compound growth as a wealth-building tool. We discuss the importance of setting financial goals, understanding risk tolerance, and diversifying investments. We also provide an overview of different investment vehicles, such as stocks, bonds, mutual funds, and real estate, and their potential returns.

Section 2: Developing an investment strategy based on individual goals and risk tolerance Here, we guide readers through the process of developing an investment strategy based on their goals and risk tolerance. We discuss the importance of asset allocation, rebalancing portfolios, and adopting a long-term perspective. We also provide insights into different investment strategies, such as value investing, growth investing, and income investing, to help readers align their investments with their objectives.

Section 3: Navigating investment platforms and working with financial professionals. In this section, we explore different investment platforms, such as online brokerages, robo-advisors, and traditional brokerage firms. We discuss the benefits and considerations of each platform and provide guidance on selecting the most suitable option based on individual needs and preferences. We also discuss the role of financial professionals, such as financial advisors or wealth managers, and provide tips on finding trustworthy and reputable professionals when seeking personalized investment guidance.

CHAPTER 14
TAX PLANNING STRATEGIES FOR FINANCIAL OPTIMIZATION

Section 1: Understanding the impact of taxes on personal finances and investments. In this section, we delve into the impact of taxes on personal finances and investments. We discuss different types of taxes, such as income tax, capital gains tax, and estate tax. We also explore tax-efficient investment strategies and techniques to minimize tax liabilities, such as utilizing tax-advantaged accounts, harvesting investment losses, and considering tax implications when rebalancing portfolios.

Section 2: Leveraging tax-advantaged accounts for retirement savings and education expenses Here, we explore the benefits of tax-advantaged accounts, such as 401(k)s, IRAs, 529 plans, and health savings accounts (HSAs). We discuss the tax advantages and contribution limits associated with each account type. We also provide guidance on how to leverage these accounts to optimize retirement savings and save for education expenses while minimizing tax burdens.

Section 3: Staying informed about changes in tax laws and seeking professional advice. In this section, we emphasize the importance of staying informed about changes in tax laws and seeking professional advice when necessary. We discuss resources for accessing up-to-date tax information, such as official government websites or tax publications. We also highlight the value of consulting with tax professionals, such as certified public accountants (CPAs) or tax attorneys, to ensure compliance with tax laws and identify potential tax-saving opportunities.

CHAPTER 15
MINDSET SHIFT: CULTIVATING A POSITIVE RELATIONSHIP WITH MONEY

Section 1: Understanding the connection between mindset and financial success. In this section, we explore the connection between mindset and financial success. We discuss the impact of limiting beliefs, self-sabotaging behaviours, and scarcity mindset on financial decisions and outcomes. We emphasize the importance of cultivating a positive relationship with money and adopting an abundance mindset to attract financial opportunities.

Section 2: Overcoming money-related fears and developing a growth mindset Here, we provide guidance on overcoming money-related fears and developing a growth mindset. We discuss common fears, such as fear of failure, fear of success, or fear of taking risks, and provide strategies to overcome them. We also explore techniques for developing resilience, embracing challenges, and viewing financial setbacks as learning opportunities.

Section 3: Practicing gratitude, mindfulness, and financial self-care. In this section, we emphasize the importance of practicing gratitude, mindfulness, and financial self-care in fostering a healthy relationship with money. We discuss the benefits of gratitude practices, such as keeping a gratitude journal or expressing gratitude for financial blessings. We also explore mindfulness techniques to cultivate awareness of financial habits and promote intentional decision-making. Additionally, we highlight the significance of self-care in managing financial stress and maintaining overall well-being.

CHAPTER 16
FINANCIAL EDUCATION FOR CHILDREN AND TEENS

Section 1: Introducing financial literacy as an essential life skill. In this section, we discuss the importance of financial literacy as an essential life skill for children and teenagers. We explore the potential long-term benefits of early financial education and the consequences of a lack of financial knowledge. We emphasize the role of parents, guardians, and educators in imparting financial skills to young individuals.

Section 2: Teaching basic money concepts and smart financial habits Here, we provide practical strategies for teaching basic money concepts and smart financial habits to children and teenagers. We discuss age-appropriate lessons on topics such as budgeting, saving, spending wisely, and distinguishing needs from wants. We also explore techniques for making financial education engaging and interactive, such as games, simulations, or real-life examples.

Section 3: Preparing for future financial success through long-term planning. In this section, we address the importance of long-term planning in preparing children and teenagers for future financial success. We discuss strategies for introducing concepts like goal-setting, investing, and career planning. We also explore the significance of teaching responsible borrowing, understanding credit, and planning for higher education expenses. By instilling these skills and knowledge early on, young individuals can develop a solid foundation for their financial well-being.

CHAPTER 17
NAVIGATING MAJOR LIFE EVENTS: FINANCIAL CONSIDERATIONS

Section 1: Financial considerations when getting married or entering a committed partnership. In this section, we discuss the financial considerations that arise when getting married or entering a committed partnership. We explore topics such as joint finances, prenuptial agreements, combining assets, and aligning financial goals. We also provide insights on how to navigate conversations about money, establish shared financial responsibilities, and plan for a financially secure future together.

Section 2: Financial considerations when starting a family or becoming a parent Here, we delve into the financial considerations that come with starting a family or becoming a parent. We discuss budgeting for childcare expenses, evaluating insurance coverage, creating an emergency fund, and planning for future educational costs. We also explore topics such as estate planning, life insurance, and ensuring financial security for children. By understanding these considerations, individuals can make informed financial decisions that support their growing families.

Section 3: Financial considerations when going through major life transitions or experiencing loss. In this section, we address the financial considerations that accompany major life transitions or experiences of loss, such as divorce, career changes, or the passing of a loved one. We discuss topics like dividing assets, navigating career transitions, managing income changes, and seeking professional guidance during challenging times. We emphasize the importance of financial resilience and adapting to new circumstances with careful planning and support.

CHAPTER 18
PHILANTHROPY AND GIVING BACK: THE POWER OF GENEROSITY

Section 1: Exploring the benefits and motivations behind philanthropy and giving back. In this section, we explore the benefits and motivations behind philanthropy and giving back. We discuss the positive impact of generosity on personal well-being, relationships, and society as a whole. We also examine different motivations for giving, such as personal values, desire for social change, or creating a lasting legacy.

Section 2: Identifying causes and organizations aligned with personal values

Here, we guide readers through the process of identifying causes and organizations that align with their personal values and interests. We discuss techniques for researching and evaluating charitable organizations, understanding their missions, and assessing their impact. We also provide insights on different ways to give back, such as volunteering time, donating money, or contributing skills and expertise.

Section 3: Maximizing the impact of philanthropic efforts and creating a giving plan. In this section, we explore strategies for maximizing the impact of philanthropic efforts and creating a giving plan. We discuss techniques such as strategic giving, collaborating with other donors or foundations, and leveraging philanthropy as a tool for social change. We also provide guidance on creating a structured giving plan, setting philanthropic goals, and measuring the outcomes of charitable contributions.

CHAPTER 19
FINANCIAL SECURITY FOR AN UNCERTAIN FUTURE

Section 1: Understanding and managing financial risks. In this section, we discuss the importance of understanding and managing financial risks to ensure long-term security. We explore different types of risks, such as market volatility, job loss, health emergencies, or natural disasters. We also provide strategies for mitigating risks through diversification, emergency planning, insurance coverage, and building financial resilience.

Section 2: Planning for retirement in an evolving landscape Here, we delve into the challenges and considerations of planning for retirement in an evolving landscape. We discuss factors such as increasing life expectancy, shifting retirement age expectations, and changing retirement savings vehicles. We also explore strategies for adapting retirement plans to account for these dynamics and maximizing retirement income sources.

Section 3: Navigating economic uncertainties and adapting financial strategies. In this section, we address the importance of navigating economic uncertainties and adapting financial strategies in response to changing circumstances. We discuss techniques for staying informed about economic trends, managing debt, maintaining a flexible financial plan, and seeking professional advice when needed. By embracing adaptability and proactive decision-making, individuals can navigate uncertainties with greater confidence and resilience.

CHAPTER 20
FINANCIAL SUCCESS AS A JOURNEY, NOT A DESTINATION

Section 1: Embracing lifelong learning and continuous improvement. In this section, we emphasize the value of lifelong learning and continuous improvement on the journey to financial success. We discuss the benefits of staying informed about personal finance, exploring new investment opportunities, and expanding financial knowledge. We also encourage readers to seek personal growth beyond financial goals and to embrace a holistic approach to well-being.

Section 2: Fostering meaningful relationships and connections. Here, we explore the significance of fostering meaningful relationships and connections on the path to financial success. We discuss the role of support networks, mentors, and accountability partners in providing guidance, motivation, and emotional support. We also highlight the importance of giving back and contributing to the well-being of others within the context of financial success.

Section 3: Embracing gratitude and celebrating milestones along the way. In this section, we encourage readers to embrace gratitude and celebrate milestones along their financial journey. We discuss the power of acknowledging progress, expressing gratitude for achievements, and finding joy in the process. We also emphasize the importance of maintaining balance, self-reflection, and self-care to sustain long-term financial success and overall well-being.

As readers progress through the chapters, they gain a comprehensive understanding of personal finance, from basic money management skills to complex investment strategies and considerations for major life events. The book aims to empower individuals to take control of their financial lives, make informed decisions, and ultimately achieve financial success and well-being.

www.ingramcontent.com/pod-product-compliance
Lightning Source LLC
Chambersburg PA
CBHW070426240526
45472CB00020B/1429